Chalking & Stamping Techniques

using scrapbooks

Karen McIvor & Sarah Mason

SEARCH PRESS

First published in Great Britain 2007

Search Press Limited
Wellwood, North Farm Road,
Tunbridge Wells, Kent TN2 3DR

Text copyright © Karen McIvor and Sarah Mason 2007

Photographs by Steve Crispe, Search Press Studios; and Roddy Paine Photographic Studio
Photographs and design copyright © Search Press Ltd 2007

All rights reserved. No part of this book, text, photographs or illustrations may be reproduced or transmitted in any form or by any means by print, photoprint, microfilm, microfiche, photocopier, internet or in any way known or as yet unknown, or stored in a retrieval system, without written permission obtained beforehand from Search Press.

ISBN-10: 1-84448-150-6
ISBN-13: 978-1-84448-150-7

The Publishers and authors can accept no responsibility for any consequences arising from the information, advice or instructions given in this publication.

Readers are permitted to reproduce any of the items/patterns in this book for their personal use, or for the purposes of selling for charity, free of charge and without the prior permission of the Publishers. Any use of the items/patterns for commercial purposes is not permitted without the prior permission of the Publishers.

Suppliers
If you have difficulty in obtaining any of the materials and equipment mentioned in this book, then please visit the Search Press website for details of suppliers:
www.searchpress.com

Every attempt has been made to contact companies who hold the copyright to the stamp designs used in this book, but in some cases this has not been possible. The authors and Publishers hope to have acknowledged all the relevant copyright holders, and to any who have been inadvertently left out we offer our sincere apologies.

Publisher's note
All the step-by-step photographs in this book feature the author, Karen McIvor, demonstrating chalking and stamping techniques. No models have been used.

Acknowledgements

I would like to thank all the friends and family who have encouraged me to be as creative as I can be. Thank you to my darling son Jack who is the main reason that I scrapbook and puts up with having his photo taken at every available opportunity. My special thanks go to my partner Dave for his unconditional love that brings out the very best in me and for picking up the slack when scrapbooking has taken over my life! And, of course, thank you to my business partner and best friend Sarah without whom half of this book wouldn't exist!
Karen

I would like to thank my husband Terry for taking care of the kids and our home while I was indulging in my passion of scrapbooking. Thanks to my friends who have loaned me their precious stash and given me inspiration, and to those people in the industry who have supported me and become like friends, particularly Barry from Ellison and Ray from Personal Impressions, without whom business would be boring! Lastly, thanks to Karen for enduring me for the last four years, crying with me, laughing with me and being like a sister.
Sarah

Many thanks indeed to the following for supplying us with many of the materials we used in the book: Banana Frog (www.bananafrog.co.uk); Blonde Moments (www.blondemoments.org); Card-io (www.card-io.co.uk); Clarity Stamps (www.claritystamp.co.uk); Dimension Fourth Ltd (www.dimensionfourthltd.co.uk); The Stamp Connection (www.thestampconnection.co.uk); Total Papercrafts (www.totalpapercrafts.co.uk); Mandy Webb, Jill Cain and Pauline Blowers.

Thank you also to the following copyright holders for allowing us to use their stamp designs: Artistic Stamper (www.theartisticstamper.com); B Line Designs; Creative Expressions (www.creative-expressions.uk.com); Creative Stamping Ltd; Ellison Design (www.ellisondesign.co.uk); HobbyCraft (www.hobbycraft.co.uk, tel. 0800 027 2387); Lakeland Limited (www.lakelandlimited.co.uk); Making Memories (www.makingmemories.com); Personal Impressions (www.richstamp.co.uk); Quickutz (www.quickutz.com); Rubber Stampede; Rubber Stamp Tapestry (www.rubberstamptapestry.com); Scrapaholic Ltd (www.scrapaholic.co.uk); Scrapgenie (www.scrapgenie.co.uk); Stampington and Company; A Stamp in the Hand Co; and Stamps Happen, Inc.

Contents

Introduction 4

Materials 6
  Papers and card 6
  Stamps 7
  Chalks 8
  Inks 8
  Embellishments 9
  Other materials and equipment 10

Techniques 12
  Simple stamping 24
  Wet embossing and stamping 26
  Ironing and stamping 28
  Soot stamping 30
  Resist stamping 32
  Dry chalking 34
  Wet chalking 36
  Alcohol inks 38
  Altered embellishments 40
  Making your own stamp 42
  Shrink plastic 44

Index 48

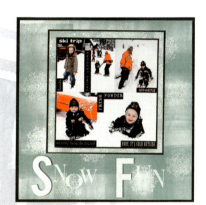

Introduction

One of the great things about scrapbooking is that it is a fantastic way of combining the various techniques and skills we learn from other crafts. Two of the most widely used ones are chalking and stamping. They can be used separately or in combination, and are a wonderful way to add colour, texture and design to any paper-based craft project.

This book includes many different ways of using chalks and stamps, starting with the basic techniques such as how to apply chalk and ink-up a stamp, and then moving on to a series of projects that incorporate a range of techniques into beautiful scrapbook page designs. All of these designs can, of course, be applied to other items, including greetings cards, gift tags and boxes, picture frames, bookmarks and notebook covers. We show you the tools that you will need, most of which are common to other crafts and are therefore widely available, and, importantly, we show you how to use the tools effectively so that you can achieve great results.

This book aims to encourage you to try out the techniques of chalking and stamping for yourself. Be imaginative, experiment, and create designs that are full of colour and interest! If you have never tried chalking and stamping before, then now is the time to grab your inks, stamps and chalks and go for it!

All of these designs can be made using the chalking and stamping techniques described in this book.

Materials

As you read through this section, you will probably recognise most, if not all, the materials and equipment we have used to design and create the scrapbook pages in this book. We have chosen items that are widely available and that most crafters may already own to encourage you to try out the techniques and projects for yourself. You certainly don't need everything that is mentioned here, and similar effects can often be created using other tools and materials. The most important thing is that you are inspired to get out what you have, or purchase a few basic items, and be creative!

Papers and card

Scrapbook pages traditionally use 30.5 x 30.5cm (12 x 12in) cardstock or paper as the basis for the design, however a number of other formats have recently grown in popularity. It is for this reason that scrapbook paper and card is now available in a number of sizes, including 15 x 15cm (6 x 6in), 20.5 x 20.5cm (8 x 8in) and 20.5 x 28cm (8 x 11in).

There is a huge range of **patterned scrapbook paper** available, with something to suit every taste, and every style and type of photograph. The most important thing to consider when choosing your patterned paper is that it complements your photographs and shows them off to their best advantage, and does not dominate the page. After all, the photographs should be the most important aspect of your scrapbooks.

Scrapbook-safe **cardstock** can now be found in a spectrum of colours and a number of different textures. It is important to be aware that textured cardstock may affect the finished result when you are stamping or chalking directly on to it, and it is worth experimenting on a scrap of textured card first. Some cardstock is produced with a white core while other types are dyed with a single colour throughout. The properties of these different types of card mean that they can be used to create very different effects. Try tearing card with a white core to produce a ragged white edge that can then be chalked or coloured with an inkpad.

As paper and card can be damaged easily, it is important that it is protected and stored away from direct sunlight, which can quickly fade the pigments within the paper. There is a huge range of storage systems available for 30.5 x 30.5cm (12 x 12in) cardstock and paper, which includes boxes that lay flat and files that stack paper vertically.

Stamps

Mounted stamps are ready to use virtually straight away with little preparation. The most commonly available mounted stamps are made of rubber and mounted on to a wooden block. The stamp usually has a layer of cushioning between the image and the wood block to enable a clear, crisp image. Wood-mounted stamps frequently have the stamp design reproduced on the top surface of the mount to help you choose the correct image for your projects. Although they tend to be more expensive than other types of stamps, wood-mounted stamps are fuss-free and easy to use.

Foam- and acrylic-mounted stamps are more recent additions to the stamp family and provide a lower-cost option. They are quite robust and can be cleaned with soap and water rather than requiring specialist products. Acrylic-mounted stamps are transparent and allow you to see exactly where the image is positioned before you stamp, which is a huge advantage over other types of mounted stamp and takes some of the guesswork out of stamping.

Unmounted stamps are purchased as sheets of images, often uncut, and therefore require a little preparation before you can start stamping with them. Because you do some of the work, the price of these stamps is considerably lower than that of mounted stamps. Unmounted stamps take up a lot less room than mounted ones if storage space is at a premium.

Unmounted stamps are available in both rubber and acrylic. Acrylic stamps are generally pre-cut and are used with an acrylic stamping block, although they will cling to any smooth, shiny surface. Unmounted rubber stamps are available in sheets containing a number of different designs, making them great value for money. These need to be combined with an adhesive cushion layer before attaching them to an acrylic block.

This die-cutting system has a stamp-making kit available so you can make your own unmounted stamps quickly and easily.

All stamps should be stored away from direct sunlight as this can cause the image to harden and crack. All stamps should be cleaned thoroughly after each use to avoid the cross-contamination of ink colours. Stamp-cleaning solutions and scrubbing pads are readily available and make cleaning a quick and simple task. Avoid soaking the cushion layer of mounted stamps as this can lead to deterioration of the foam. Allow your stamps to dry thoroughly before they are stored. Unmounted stamps can be stored on plastic sheets in file folders for a low-cost, space-saving option.

Chalks

Chalks are available in a number of different forms, including individual chalks, mini palettes and colour-themed sets. There is something to suit all budgets and personal preferences. Some of the newest chalks, called shimmer chalks, come with a shimmer effect that can be burnished to create an eye-catching sparkle.

Chalks are dry, concentrated pigment in a soft block that require some form of applicator to use them effectively. Foam applicators with a soft foam tip allow you to add colour precisely within a small area. Crocodile-clip applicators are used with pompoms, available in various sizes for a number of different uses. Try using brushes and cotton wool as well for a variety of effects.

Chalks are brittle and can smash easily if dropped or handled roughly. Treat chalks with care to minimise the risk of damage. Use a clean applicator for each colour of chalk to avoid cross-contamination of colours.

Inks

Inks are a wet pigment that will dry at a certain rate depending on the ingredients of the ink. The different drying rates of different types of inkpad can be used to create different effects, including embossing and 'kissing off' (see page 20).

Dye-based inks dry quickly, allowing you to work fast with little risk of smudging your stamped image. **Embossing inks** are slower to dry, allowing you time to add embossing powder and heat-set them. **Chalk inks** dry to a flat, dull finish similar to chalk but with a more intense colour. **Solvent-based inks**

dry quickly and adhere to most surfaces, including glass and metal. **Alcohol inks** are new on the scene and can be dripped on to projects or applied with a pad for a number of different effects. The colour is suspended in alcohol, which evaporates quickly to leave an intense shot of colour on most surfaces, including plastic and metal.

All inkpads are at risk of drying out and many manufacturers produce re-inkers that can be used to refresh an inkpad. To minimise the risk of drying out, replace the lid on your inkpads immediately after use. Storing inkpads upside down brings the available ink to the upper surface of the pad, prolonging their lifespan. Alcohol inks can evaporate quickly so be sure to screw the caps on tightly and store them upright to prevent spillages.

Embellishments

Almost anything can be used to embellish a scrapbook page – the only limitation is your own imagination. Products offered by scrapbook manufacturers are guaranteed to be archival and safe to use next to your photographs, but there might be other items you want to include on a page to set the theme. Paper-based items such as programmes, tickets and postcards can be treated with a preservation spray that will stop deterioration of the paper and make them safe to use. Some purists will not include anything that is not guaranteed to be safe on their pages, while others throw caution to the wind and include anything that takes their fancy regardless of its potential to damage their photographs. The important thing is to be able to make an informed decision.

The designs in this book use a wide range of embellishments, usually products that are archival. Ribbons and trimmings are safe to use as long as they are fabric and do not include metallic threads or wire edges. Likewise, fabric and paper flowers can be used to add a soft, romantic or feminine touch to a design. Paint is another way to add colour to your pages, and acrylic paint is safe and easy to use. Acrylic paints from scrapbooking manufacturers have a lower water content than usual to reduce the risk of the underlying card or paper swelling and buckling.

You can add titles and journaling with alphabet stickers, word stickers, metal letters, acrylic alphabets, rub-on lettering and journaling pens. Check that stickers are acid- and lignin-free to be sure that they will look good for the lifespan of your scrapbook pages and are safe to use.

Add sparkle to your designs with glitter, either in the form of a loose powder or suspended in an adhesive for easy application. Charms can also be used to add a touch of sparkle and these are available in a huge variety of shapes and sizes to suit any style or theme.

There is a huge range of storage solutions available for embellishments, suitable for every budget and type of space. The most important thing is that you are able to quickly find what you want, when you want it. Organising by colour, type of product or size are just some options that may work for you, though the choice is very much a personal one. Embellishments should be stored out of direct sunlight to reduce the risk of colours fading. Small embellishments such as eyelets, brads and charms are best stored in containers with tight-fitting lids to prevent spillages.

Other materials and equipment

We have a basic toolkit that we use every time we design or create a scrapbook page, and we recommend that you have each of these items to hand when making the projects on pages 24–47. It includes a 30.5cm (12in) **trimmer** or **guillotine**; **scissors** in a range of sizes, both straight and decal edge; **adhesives** in the form of 3D foam pads, glue dots, glue sticks and repositionable adhesive; a **craft knife** and a **self-healing cutting mat**. Use dry adhesives such as tabs and dots to attach photographs, mounts and cardstock layers to minimise the risk of the paper fibres swelling and buckling. 3D foam pads allow you to lift a layer up in order to add dimension. Embellishments made from materials such as metal and wood will require stronger adhesives such as metal glue or glazes to ensure that they remain firmly attached to the page.

Like most crafters, we have amassed a huge range of tools and equipment over time and have used our favourites to create the designs in this book. We use **punches** and **die-cutting systems** to create crisp, cleanly cut titles and decorative elements for our layouts. A small die-cutting machine is relatively inexpensive, and alphabet dies can be found in a huge range of fonts allowing you to choose those that fit with your personal style. A punch is a versatile tool, used to create simple shapes that can be decorated and combined with others to produce a truly personal embellishment.

A **heat gun** is essential for setting embossing powder and creating a beautiful, raised embossed image quickly. A **brayer** is similar to a paint roller but is much smaller. Use this to apply paint or ink to your pages quickly and smoothly.

A range of **brushes** and **applicators** can be used for a number of different types of medium. Foam-tipped applicators allow you to apply chalks with precision and can be washed clean simply with soap and water. A paintbrush can be used for paint, but a dry paintbrush can also be used to create a soft,

cloudy chalk effect. A colour duster resembles a mini shaving brush and can be used to apply chalk to large areas quickly. Try using a colour duster together with an inkpad for a more intense colour effect. A stamp applicator has a hook fastening surface and is used with a felt pad to apply alcohol inks and more.

A **spray bottle** is used to apply a fine mist of water or other liquid medium, such as diluted ink or paint, over a surface. Be sure to clean the bottle thoroughly after use to keep the spray nozzle clear. Chalk smudges easily, so a light coating of **fixative** or **hairspray** will help protect your work once it is completed.

Stamp cleaner makes cleaning up a breeze. It is available in a spray bottle and also as an applicator pad that cleans and scrubs in one action. Some types of inkpad require a specialist cleaner; check the packaging for details.

We always have a bottle of **adhesive remover** to hand. This allows us to reposition elements on a page and to clean off patches of adhesive where it is not wanted. **Chalk enhancer** is a liquid medium that can be mixed with dry chalk to create a liquid colour. This can then be applied with a brush or foam applicator. The chalk block remains unchanged by the use of chalk enhancer once it has dried.

Techniques

This section will take you step by step through the stamping and chalking techniques we have used to create the projects in this book. It is designed to be a reference section that you will come back to from time to time for both inspiration and advice. We have included scrapbook pages throughout to show you how you can apply the techniques, and hopefully to give you ideas for making scrapbook layouts and other paper-based designs of your own.

Hula Girl
A black and white patterned paper was given a shot of colour using chalks to highlight the design on the paper and create a fun page that complements the theme of the photographs. The title was stamped with white acrylic paint and the centre sections of each letter were coloured using chalks to coordinate the page.

Applying chalk

Chalking allows you to add soft layers of colour to your designs, which can be blended together to create new shades and tones. No other colour medium offers as many options or is as versatile as chalk. The effects you are able to achieve tend to be more subtle than those obtained with other mediums such as paints and inks, providing you with almost limitless scope to be creative.

Tip
Do not apply chalk with your fingers – the oils in your skin can react with the dry chalk and create a patchy effect that cannot be removed.

Applying chalk to paper and card

Foam applicators resemble make-up sponges and are used in much the same way. They are cheap and easy to clean after use, making them a popular choice. Many chalk sets come with foam applicators as standard.

1. Pick up the chalk by swiping the foam pad across the block.

2. Apply the chalk to the card in a smooth, circular motion.

Pompoms are small cotton balls available in a range of sizes. The smaller the pompom, the more precisely you can apply the chalk. Pompoms are held with a crocodile-clip applicator and can be washed with soap and water and reused repeatedly.

1. Hold the pompom using a crocodile-clip applicator and rub the pompom on the chalk in a circular motion.

2. Dab the chalk on to the card.

A regular soft **paintbrush** can be used in a similar way to a foam applicator, but gives a softer, cloudier finish.

1. Pick up the chalk by brushing the block firmly with the brush.

2. Apply the chalk to the card using small, circular motions.

A **colour duster** resembles a mini shaving brush and is used to cover large areas quickly. It gives an even colour across the paper surface.

1. Pick up the chalk by agitating the brush on the surface of the block.

2. Apply the chalk by rubbing the brush firmly backwards and forwards.

Cotton wool in the shape of balls or pads is a cheap and fast way to add chalk to your projects. The large surface area of the cotton wool makes it ideal for covering large areas with colour.

1. Pick up the chalk by rubbing the cotton wool firmly on the block.

2. Rub the chalk on to the card using circular motions. Blow away any excess chalk dust as you work.

Applying chalk to a stamp

Chalks can be combined with other materials to create new ways to add colour to your designs. This technique uses a stamp and clear pigment ink as a carrier for dry chalk, which is then stamped on to the paper or card. The chalk colour is intensified by the pigment ink and produces a distressed or aged effect that is perfect for a heritage theme or a 'shabby chic' look.

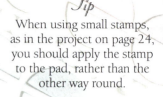

Tip
When using small stamps, as in the project on page 24, you should apply the stamp to the pad, rather than the other way round.

1. Apply a clear pigment inkpad to the rubber stamp. Make sure the pigment is applied evenly all over the entire surface of the stamp.

2. Pick up the chalk using a pompom attached to a crocodile-clip applicator.

3. Dab the chalk on to the stamp, picking out the parts of the stamp you wish to colour. Stamp the chalked image on to card or paper for a distressed image.

Using a stencil

Stencils have been used for many years to define patterns and designs and create a regular image. This technique uses a standard craft punch to make a stencil, which is then used to create a soft chalked image. Try using a die-cutting machine to cut out shapes or letters and use the negative space left behind as a stencil.

1. Cut out the stencil from a piece of card using a craft punch.

2. Lay the stencil on a piece of card and apply chalk using a foam applicator. Hold the stencil firmly in place, and work from the outside of the shape inwards, overlapping the edge of the stencil slightly. Blow away any excess chalk dust as you work.

3. Gently lift off the stencil to reveal the image underneath.

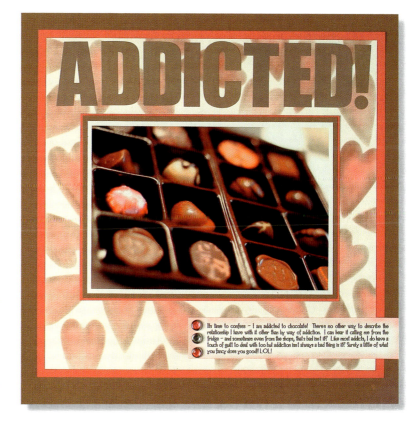

Addicted!

A stencil was randomly placed on to a sheet of white cardstock and combined with two colours of chalk to create this unique patterned background. Brown and pink cardstock and alphabet stickers were all that were needed to complete the page.

Stamping

Stamping images on to paper or card is one of the fastest and simplest ways to add pattern and colour. The range of stamps available is huge, with something to suit all styles and personal preferences. In this section we will show you how to stamp with paint and ink, how to mount an unmounted stamp and how to add another pattern to a plain stamp using the 'kissing off' technique.

Using a foam stamp

Foam stamps can be used with either inkpads or paint, but the slightly porous surface of the foam makes them a perfect partner for acrylic paint. It is easy to achieve great stamped effects with paint and foam stamps and cleaning up is as simple as running them under a tap.

1. Put a small amount of paint on to a piece of scrap card and dab it lightly with a foam brush.

2. Dab the paint evenly on to the stamp.

Dirt

Foam stamps and acrylic paint were used to create the 'DIRT' title on this page. Stamping directly on to a completed page may seem a little daunting but a pencil guideline can help to keep everything aligned. Fill in any areas that did not stamp cleanly with a fine paintbrush and a little paint.

3. Place the stamp on to the card and apply even pressure.

4. Carefully lift off the stamp to reveal the image underneath.

Using a rubber stamp

Rubber stamps can be used with any type of inkpad. The different ink types can create different effects and can make the same image look very different. Rubber stamps work better with ink than with paint as the hard rubber surface can tend to act like a 'squeegee' and push the paint off the image.

As a general rule you will achieve the best results if you apply the inkpad to the surface of the stamp rather than the other way round. This method allows you to see clearly which areas of the stamp have ink on them, and prevents you from under- or over-inking parts of the stamp, causing the image to be blurred.

Love

Dye-based inks in coordinating colours were used to stamp a number of themed words on to both plain and patterned card to create title blocks for this design. These were cut out and mounted on to dark cardstock which were then mixed with small-scale photographs and designs trimmed from the patterned paper to create a collage effect.

1. Apply the ink to the stamp by dabbing the inkpad on the stamp.

2. Place the stamp on to the card and press down firmly and evenly.

3. Carefully lift off the stamp to reveal the image underneath.

Mounting an unmounted stamp

Unmounted stamp sheets are the most cost-effective way to purchase stamps, and they are easy to store as they take up considerably less room than mounted stamps. As well as the unmounted stamp, you will need a sheet of mounting foam, a pair of sharp scissors and an acrylic stamping block.

1. Cut out the stamp using a pair of sharp scissors, leaving a narrow border around the outside of the design.

2. Cut out a piece of mounting foam slightly larger than the stamp and peel off the backing.

3. Attach the stamp to the adhesive side of the mounting foam and cut off the excess.

4. Mount the stamp on an acrylic block.

The Smiths

Stamps were used to create a decorative border around the photo mount on this page, highlighting the stamped-effect patterned paper used as a base for the design. The resulting effect sets the tone of the page and is in keeping with the era of the photograph.

Kissing off

'Kissing off' is a technique that uses two stamps together to apply a pattern to an otherwise plain stamp. A slow-drying pigment inkpad is used to allow time to add the patterned image to the plain stamp before it is stamped on to card. Mixing patterned and plain stamps using this technique can provide endless design options and extend the creative opportunities offered by your stamp collection.

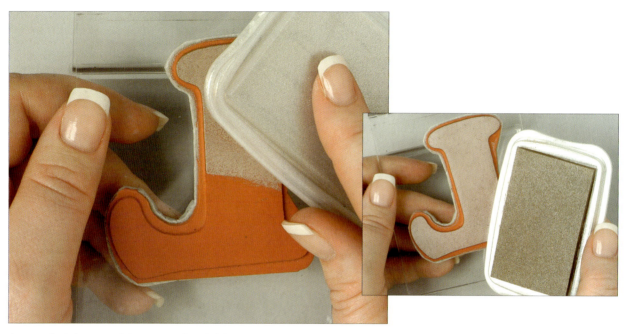

1. Apply ink to a plain stamp by dabbing the stamp with a pigment inkpad.

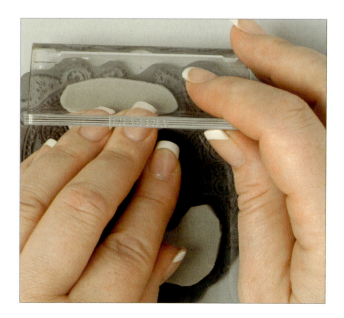

2. Take the inked, plain stamp, and press it down firmly on to a patterned stamp.

3. Lift off the plain stamp carefully. The pattern will be transferred to the inked surface.

4. Apply the patterned image to a piece of card.

Sweet Sixteen

A kissed-off stamped image was used as a monogram on this vintage-look layout. The image was stamped on to light-coloured card and then carefully trimmed to give a narrow border around the design. This was attached to the page using 3D foam pads to add dimension to the page.

Even when the same products and techniques are used, the finished results can be very different. Here we both used exactly the same products, the same stamping technique and the same types of embellishment to create our pages, but different photographs and personal styles meant that the completed layouts had totally different looks to them.

Grandparents
Sarah stamped large monograms for the initial letters of her title using a soft chalk inkpad to complement the gentle, relaxed feel of the photograph.

A Special Moment

Karen stamped on to cardstock before using it to die-cut her title letters. A simple rose stamp was stamped and embossed with glitter to create a romantic embellishment that is also a mini book of journaling.

Simple stamping

Tapestry stamps are a beautiful way of creating a collage of flowers that looks different every time you use them. By simply varying the colours used, you can change your designs to suit your project. The stamps we've used here are available in sets, and have a long wooden mount that can be held firmly in the hand like a pen. One stamp can be used to create three or more shades of the same colour depending on the number of images you stamp before re-inking. Remember that dye-based inks dry quickly, so you will have to work fast. Rather than using patterned paper, we created a uniquely patterned background using floral stamps and ink colours that complement the summer photographs perfectly. We wanted to create a natural feel to the stamping and so opted to overlay the images randomly.

You will need
Two photographs
Selection of floral tapestry rubber stamps
Alphabet foam stamps
Dye-based inkpads in shades of green, pink, lilac, light red and light orange
Two sheets of white and one of black cardstock, 30.5 x 30.5cm (12 x 12in)
Selection of small paper flowers
Decorative brads
Sheet of scrap card

Remember
You will need the basic toolkit of trimmer or guillotine (optional), scissors, adhesives, craft knife and cutting mat for each of the projects in this book (see page 10 for more details).

1. Lay the white cardstock over a sheet of scrap card. Apply the largest stamp to the pink inkpad and transfer several images to the top left-hand corner of the card in a random pattern. Stamp some of the images so that they lie partly off the edge of the card.

2. Change to the second largest stamp and a different-coloured inkpad, and place images in between those already on the sheet. Repeat with the third stamp. Use the same stamp twice, if you wish, with a different colour each time.

3. Complete the design using the remaining stamps and coloured inks. Make sure there are no obvious gaps in the pattern.

Debden

We used white cardstock as the base for this layout, creating the background stamping using the method described above. Two flower-themed photographs were mounted on to white card, trimmed to produce a narrow border, and then double-mounted on to black card, again with a narrow border. Both photographs were then adhered to the page, one slightly overlapping the other. We stamped a large title around the top right-hand corner of the main photograph and placed some paper flowers above it, secured with decorative brads. The journaling was printed out on the computer to fit the white space in the bottom left-hand corner of the page, mounted on to black card and attached to the layout.

Wet embossing and stamping

Wet embossing involves stamping an image, adding an embossing powder and then heat setting it to create a raised image. It is a simple way to create titles or decorative elements for your scrapbook pages.

By choosing different colours of embossing powders, you can create a variety of different looks with the same stamps. The example here uses a white embossing powder with a matt finish to resemble snow. In order to keep the focus on the photograph, we chose wintry shades of blue and white and combined them with a simple title that summed up the theme of the picture completely.

You will need
Photograph
Snowflake and alphabet rubber stamps
Acrylic stamping block
White embossing powder
Clear embossing inkpad
Brown chalk inkpad
Light blue and white cardstock, each 30.5 x 30.5cm (12 x 12in)
Distressed-effect blue patterned paper, 30.5 x 30.5cm (12 x 12in)
Blue/white snowflake-patterned paper in the same size
Ribbon
3D foam pads
Heat gun

1. Apply clear embossing ink to the snowflake stamp, and place a number of images in a random pattern over the top part of the blue cardstock.

2. Mount the 'S' on the acrylic block, apply the clear embossing ink to it and stamp over the snowflake background. (Using a clear block allows you to see the snowflakes through the stamp, making it easier to position.)

3. Stamp the remaining letters in the same way, leaving plenty of space between them.

4. Sprinkle the stamped images with white embossing powder.

5. Shake off the excess powder and tip it back into the pot.

6. Heat the images with a heat gun to set the embossing powder. Don't overheat, otherwise the embossing powder will start to melt down into the paper.

7. Cut out each letter using either a guillotine or a pair of scissors. They should measure approximately 3 x 5cm (1¼ x 2in).

Snow!

To create this page, we used distressed-effect patterned paper as the main background. We cut a large mount for the photograph from white cardstock and distressed the edges by brushing over them using a brown chalk inkpad. This is known as the direct-to-paper inking technique. It creates a soft, powdery finish that is perfect for a distressed or aged look.

We cut a piece of snowflake-patterned paper to the same size as the photograph and rotated it through 90° to produce an offset mount on the right of the background. Lengths of ribbon were glued along the bottom of the photograph and down the right-hand side.

Next we made the title letters using the method described above and mounted them on to white card, trimming to give a narrow border. A single snowflake was also cut out and mounted. The title letters and snowflake were then attached to the page using 3D foam pads to give a sense of dimension to the overall design.

Ironing and stamping

Stamping on to velvet using an ornate stamp can produce a really wonderful embossed effect. It allows you to add a three-dimensional look to your scrapbook pages, whilst giving your design a soft and subtle elegance. By choosing different colours of craft velvet, you can create various images that stand out on the page. In the example here we chose cream velvet to bring out the creamy tones of the sepia photograph, and a stamp with an ornate design in keeping with the Victorian theme.

You will need
Photograph
Ornate corner stamp
Cream-coloured craft velvet
White and black cardstock, each 30.5 x 30.5cm (12 x 12in)
Blue heritage-patterned paper, 30.5 x 30.5cm (12 x 12in)
Small metal alphabet letters
Narrow cream ribbon
Iron
Corner punch
Journaling pen
Small spray bottle

1. Cut out four pieces of paper-backed velvet, slightly larger than the stamp. Dampen one piece by spraying it evenly with water using a spray bottle.

2. Lay the velvet face-down on the rubber stamp. Ensure the whole image is covered and in the centre.

3. Press the velvet with a medium-hot iron. Hold the iron down firmly on the velvet for five to ten seconds (larger areas can be worked in sections).

4. Allow the velvet to cool slightly, then carefully remove it from the stamp. Repeat for the remaining three corners.

5. Trim around the edge of the design using a pair of scissors.

Chalmers

To create this page, we used a sheet of heritage-patterned paper as the main background. We double-mounted the photograph on to white card and then on to black card, leaving a thin, even border each time. Using a corner punch, we punched out four corners from the craft velvet and wrapped them around each corner of the mounted photograph.

The title of the page, spelt out in metal letters, was attached to the ribbon, which was then wrapped and glued around the mount. We then triple-mounted the photograph on to white card, ensuring a wide, even border. The date the photograph was taken was written on the outer white border in the bottom left-hand corner.

We attached the mounted photograph to the centre of the background card, then created four iron-stamped corner images on cream-coloured craft velvet using the method described above and adhered them to the corners.

Soot stamping

Soot stamping is an unusual way to use your stamps. The technique involves removing soot with a stamp to reveal the colour of the card underneath. In this way, a 'negative' image of your stamp is produced on a dark, cloudy background. It can be tricky to produce perfect results straight away, but if you practise a little first with some scrap card, you will quickly grasp the technique.

Beach pictures do not necessarily need to be given a traditional beach theme. In this design we have combined orange and black to create an eye-catching scrapbook page. The elements were arranged in the top left- and bottom right-hand corners to draw the eye diagonally across the page to the photograph.

You will need
Photograph
Flower rubber stamp
Acrylic stamping block
Orange chalk block and applicator
White and black cardstock, each 30.5 x 30.5cm (12 x 12in)
Orange patterned paper, 30.5 x 30.5cm (12 x 12in)
Assorted ribbons and trimmings
Two orange brads
Candle and matches
Absorbent paper
Spray fixative or hairspray
3D foam pads

1. Light the candle. Roll the card in two and hold it in the tip of the flame. The soot will transfer to the card. Move the card constantly to obtain an even coating of soot, and to prevent the card from catching fire.

2. Mount the stamp on the acrylic block and stamp the design on to the soot in a random pattern. The stamp lifts off the soot, leaving an imprint of the image behind. Clean the stamp with slightly damp absorbent paper after stamping every two or three images.

3. When you have covered an area approximately 15 x 30.5cm (6 x 12in), spray it lightly and evenly with fixative or hairspray to prevent smudging.

XOXO

A sheet of back cardstock was used as the base for this design. We then trimmed off the edges of a sheet of orange patterned paper and attached it over the base card, leaving a narrow black border. The soot-stamped card was trimmed to 28cm (11in) wide and torn to produce a strip 7.5cm (3in) high. This was then attached across the bottom of the background paper. We attached strips of ribbon and trimmings horizontally and vertically on the page, and a monogram letter was cut from the remaining soot-stamped card and attached over the top left-hand corner of the photograph using 3D foam pads. We printed journaling on to white card and coloured the edges using orange chalk applied with an applicator. The journaling strip was adhered to the page and secured with two orange brads.

Resist stamping

Resist stamping involves stamping an image, adding an embossing powder and then heating it to create a raised image. A layer of ink is then rolled over it to make the image stand out from the page. It is a simple way of creating your own patterned background papers using different colours of embossing powder, coordinating ink and stamps. The example here uses a white embossing powder with a grey background, reminiscent of snow and grey clouds.

You will need
Photographs
Snowflake rubber stamp
White and black cardstock, each 30.5 x 30.5cm (12 x 12in)
Clear embossing inkpad
Clear embossing powder
Grey pigment-based inkpad
Word stickers or label maker
Metal monogram letters
Rub-on alphabet letters
Heat gun
Brayer

1. Apply the rubber stamp to the clear embossing inkpad and stamp the image in a random pattern over the white cardstock.

2. Sprinkle clear embossing powder over the sheet. Tip the excess back in to the pot.

3. Heat the stamped images with a heat gun until the powder turns glossy. Do not overheat, otherwise the powder will start to melt into the card.

4. Ink up the brayer using a grey pigment-based inkpad and roll it over the card, changing direction at regular intervals. The ink adheres to the card, but not to the embossed images.

The completed design. You do not need to ink the central part of the card as this will be covered by the photograph.

Snow Fun

To create this page, we trimmed 2.5cm (1in) from two adjoining sides of the patterned background (made using the method described above) and mounted it centrally on to black card. This was repeated with a smaller piece of white card, this time stamping the images closer to the edges. We used this for the photo mount. We made a collage of photographs and mounted them on to black card leaving a thin, even border. We then placed themed word stickers, horizontally and vertically, on each photograph. (A label maker can be used if you cannot find themed stickers.) The photographs were then double-mounted on to the patterned mount created earlier leaving a wide, even border so that the pattern underneath was clearly visible. This was then triple-mounted on to black card leaving a thin, even border. The photographs were then placed centrally in the upper part of the background card, leaving sufficient space underneath for the title.

We chose a white metal monogram for the first letter of each word in the title and embossed the background image on to it to carry the theme through. Each word was then completed using rub-on alphabet letters.

Dry chalking

Dry chalking is the simplest of the chalking techniques and involves simply rubbing chalk over the surface of the paper. In this project we used crumpled tissue paper and shimmer chalks to add texture and colour to the page title. This technique works better with strong, bold chalk colours but a more delicate effect can be created if the base card is painted white before you start. Start by photocopying the title letter template on this page and enlarging it by fifty per cent.

The colourful books in the background of the photograph set the theme for this page, which suits perfectly the age of the subject. We used a song lyric for the title as it captured everything we wanted to say. Songs, poems and quotes are great sources for both titles and journaling for scrapbooks.

You will need
Photograph
Shimmer chalks
Pompoms and crocodile-clip applicator
Orange, pink and cream cardstock, each 30.5 x 30.5cm (12 x 12in)
Spotted paper, 30.5 x 30.5cm (12 x 12in)
Squared paper in the same size
Template for the letters
Sheet of thick card
Sheet of crumpled white tissue paper
Green and orange twill
Three brass picture hangers
Six brads
White rub-on lettering
Glue stick

1. Cut out each of the letters from thick card using the template. Apply glue to the top surface of one of the letters using a glue stick.

Templates for the letters, two-thirds actual size.

2. Cut out a piece of crumpled tissue paper so that it is slightly larger than the shape you wish to cover, and stick it over the card letter.

3. Fold the sides of the tissue paper underneath the shape and glue them down.

4. Apply shimmer chalk using a pompom held in a crocodile-clip applicator.

Colours

We used a sheet of cream card as the base of this design, overlaying it with a sheet of orange card that had been trimmed slightly to create an even border. Blocks of patterned paper were then layered over the base so that they overlapped each other. The photograph was mounted on to pink card, offset to leave a large border on the right-hand side.

Each of the title letters was coloured with a different chalk. We also made a set of parentheses and coloured them in the same way. The title letters and parentheses were attached to the page using glue dots. We then attached three brass picture hangers to the bottom left-hand corner of the design using brads, and tied short lengths of twill through them. Finally we cut a decorative corner out of patterned paper and attached it to the bottom right-hand corner of the layout, then used white rub-on lettering to complete the title.

Wet chalking

Wet chalking has more impact than chalking directly on to card. By simply adding a small amount of chalk enhancer or water you can create a bolder statement on your scrapbook page and bring in colours that match your photograph perfectly. We drew inspiration from the lines of the shopping basket in the photograph for the chalked lines on this page, but don't be limited by straight lines; try using stencils and masks to create your own unique background.

You will need
Photograph
Chalk blocks
Foam applicator
White cardstock, 30.5 x 30.5cm (12 x 12in)
Blue cardstock, 16 x 22cm (6¼ x 8¾in)
Green cardstock, 15.5 x 21.5cm (6 x 8½in)
Large light brown alphabet stickers
Medium light green alphabet stickers
Small container of chalk enhancer or water
Spray adhesive
Metal ruler

1. First make the mount for the photograph by attaching the blue card to the green using acid-free repositionable spray adhesive. Attach the mount to the centre of the white cardstock. Lay a ruler approximately 1cm (½in) below the mount. This is where you will place the first line of the bottom right-hand design.

2. Dampen the foam applicator, pick up some green chalk and draw a straight line below the right-hand side of the picture mount, and extending a little way beyond it.

3. Draw a longer line underneath and two more vertical ones in the pattern shown above. Chalk dries very quickly, so you do not need to worry about smudging the lines you have drawn previously.

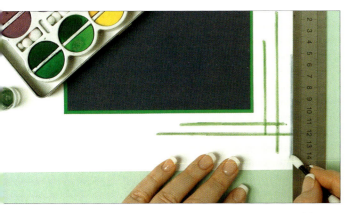
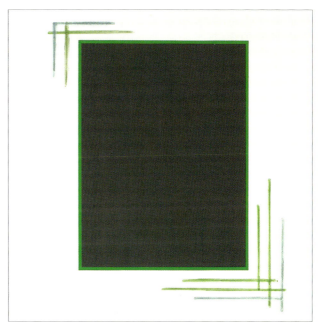

4. Draw another vertical line, this time using blue chalk. Join the vertical line with a horizontal line to create an L shape under the green.

5. Add a similar, smaller design to the top left-hand corner of the picture mount.

Simply Lucas

We used white card as a base for this layout and followed the steps above to create the central mount. We then attached the photograph. Using the large, light brown letters, we spelt out the name 'Lucas' in the bottom left-hand corner of the mount. We completed the title using the smaller, light green letters and wrote the date of the photograph in the right-hand corner under the green mount.

Alcohol inks

Clear buttons may never really have appealed to crafters until the introduction of alcohol inks! Alcohol inks come in a range of vivid, transparent colours and have a wide variety of effects depending on the surface you use them on. Plastic, metal, glass and any type of non-absorbent surface can be coloured using alcohol inks, producing a fantastic mottled effect. The inks dry quickly and can be easily removed using acetone. Alcohol inks can also be used on paper and card.

We created fun, colourful buttons for this page to reflect the outgoing and bubbly personality of the girl in the photograph.

You will need
Photograph
Flat metal stamp applicator
Small piece of hook-and-loop fastener and a small piece of felt
Alcohol inks in green, purple and dark pink
Cream, pink and light blue cardstock, each 30.5 x 30.5cm (12 x 12in)
Green spotted paper, 30.5 x 30.5cm (12 x 12in)
Mixed floral-patterned paper in the same size
Five clear acrylic buttons
Length of lilac-coloured twill
Yellow embroidery floss
Chipboard letters
Decorative rub-ons
3D foam pads
Corner punch

1. Attach the hook side of a strip of hook-and-loop fastener to a flat stamp, then place a piece of felt over it to make the applicator for the alcohol inks.

2. Drop three spots of alcohol ink – one of each colour – on the felt. Overlap them so they blend slightly.

 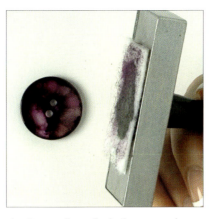 

3. Place one of the acrylic buttons on a sheet of scrap card and stamp it two or three times in quick succession, changing the angle of the stamp each time.

4. Cover the whole button, then stamp a second layer of ink. The first layer will have dried slightly, so the second layer sticks to it, creating a mottled effect.

Three finished buttons.

Lori

This page was created with a sheet of pink cardstock as a base. We then cut a piece of green spotted paper and a piece of light blue cardstock, and rounded the corners with a punch before attaching them to the background. Rounding the corners of the photograph as well, we mounted it on to the cream card and trimmed around the border, making it wider along the bottom edge.

The ends of the length of twill were tied together in a double knot and trimmed before wrapping it around the bottom of the photo mount. Flowers were then cut from the patterned paper and attached to the page; some were lifted off the background using 3D foam pads.

We threaded yellow floss through the holes in two of the buttons and tied it on the right side in a double knot. The ends were trimmed and frayed before attaching the buttons over the centres of the larger flowers. Three further buttons were coloured using alcohol inks and floss tied through their centres. Further decoration was added using a chipboard title and rub-ons.

Altered embellishments

Embellishments are a great way to decorate your scrapbook pages, and altering them makes them much more personal. This technique combines both stamping and chalking to alter clear acrylic buttons, making unique coordinating embellishments. Solvent-based inkpads will stamp on to non-porous surfaces such as plastic, creating a permanent image that will not smudge off.

Soft and feminine colours were chosen here to produce pretty embellishments that complement the floral paper and create a baby-themed page. Varying the colours and stamp designs used produces very different results that can complement a broad range of styles of photograph.

You will need
Photograph
Simple flower acrylic stamp
Acrylic stamping block
White solvent-based inkpad
Chalk blocks
Pompoms and crocodile-clip applicator
Cream cardstock, 30.5 x 30.5cm (12 x 12in)
Green spotted paper, 30.5 x 30.5cm (12 x 12in)
Mixed floral-patterned paper in the same size
Five or six clear acrylic buttons
White alphabet stickers
Assorted fabric and paper flowers
Coloured brads
Monogram letter
Small tag
Cream-coloured embroidery thread
Two coloured photo turns

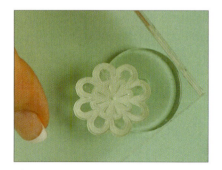

1. Mount the stamp on the acrylic block. Apply white solvent-based ink before stamping the image on to one of the acrylic buttons.

2. Allow the ink to dry before applying coloured chalk to the stamped image using a pompom held in a crocodile-clip applicator.

3. Turn the button over so that the image is on the underside before attaching it to your page.

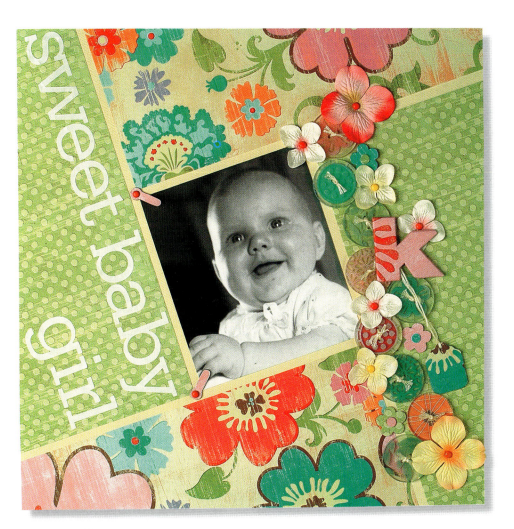

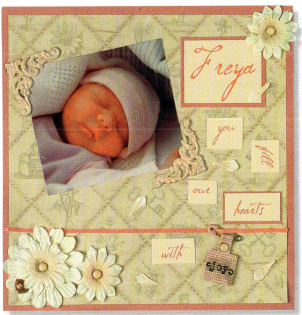

Sweet Baby Girl

For this layout we used a base of cream cardstock, and attached a photograph in the centre at an angle on the page. We then attached alternating sections of patterned paper around the photograph, and secured a pink photo turn at each of its left-hand corners. Fabric flowers and buttons were arranged in a random pattern down the right-hand side of the photograph, tying embroidery thread through the centres of the buttons first. The buttons were attached using adhesive, and the flowers were secured to the page with coloured brads.

A monogram letter and a small tag were covered with off-cuts of the floral-patterned paper and attached to the page. We completed the design with a title created using white alphabet stickers.

Freya

The paper flowers on this page were delicately coloured using pastel chalks. The ornate photo corners were originally metal. We painted them with cream acrylic paint and altered them further by rubbing them with shimmer chalk to highlight the pattern.

Making your own stamp

Making your own stamps can be quick and easy using a die-cutting system and some adhesive-backed foam. There are numerous shapes to choose from, so you will easily find something that matches the theme of your layout. If you don't have a die-cutting machine, try printing an image on the computer and tracing it on to foam, then cutting the shape out by hand. Foam is an inexpensive way to create your own stamps and is versatile enough to be used with all types of inks and paints.

We used a classic stamp design to produce a 22.5 x 22.5cm (8 x 8in) format page that is simple and sophisticated. The pink cardstock and flowers were chosen to emphasise the feminine theme of the design.

You will need
Photographs
Die-cutting machine and die
Strip of stamping foam
Acrylic stamping block
Pink and white cardstock, each 30.5 x 30.5cm (12 x 12in)
Black cardstock, 22.5 x 22.5cm (8 x 8in)
White acrylic paint
Foam brush
Pink ribbon
Pink paper flowers (four or five small and one large)
Decorative brad
Glitter glue
Decorative rub-ons

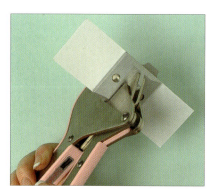

1. Place the die upside-down in the die cutter with the piece of stamping foam underneath. Squeeze down firmly on the cutter.

2. Remove the cut-out image from the stamping foam.

3. Remove the paper backing and attach the foam stamp to the acrylic block.

4. Apply white acrylic paint to the stamp using a foam brush and transfer the image to one corner of the black card.

5. Continue stamping the image on the black card, reapplying paint to the stamp each time.

Precious Memories

This scrapbook page was created using a sheet of pink cardstock as a base. We produced the background following the method described above and attached it to the lower part of the page, adding a piece of pink ribbon to cover the join. Our chosen photographs were mounted on to white, pink and black card and decorated in one corner with small paper flowers, adding glitter glue to the centres as a finishing touch. Once the photographs had been attached to the base, we added decorative rub-ons, and a large flower to the bottom left-hand corner secured with a brad.

Shrink plastic

Once you have been bitten by the stamping bug, you may find yourself looking for new surfaces to stamp on. Stamping on to shrink plastic is easy and, after shrinking, produces a smaller-scale version of your stamped image. This technique gives you the opportunity to use your stamps in a different way to produce an eye-catching finished result. Start by photocopying the title template on this page and doubling it in size to produce a full-size template that is ready to use.

Mixing type styles is a great way to add visual interest to a title, and can use up left-over stickers and alphabet letters.

You will need
Photograph
Rubber background stamp
Pigment-based inkpads in blue and purple
White and brown cardstock, each 30.5 x 30.5cm (12 x 12in)
Striped paper, 30.5 x 30.5cm (12 x 12in)
Green floral-patterned paper in the same size
Blue floral-patterned paper in the same size
Templates for the letters
Sheet of shrink plastic
Die-cut tags
White alphabet stickers
Paper flower
Guillotine and/or scissors
Black and white rub-on lettering
Large pair of tweezers
Heat gun

Templates for the letters, half actual size.

1. Apply pigment ink to the stamp. Use first one inkpad and then the other to obtain a variegated effect.

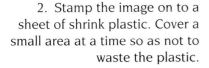

2. Stamp the image on to a sheet of shrink plastic. Cover a small area at a time so as not to waste the plastic.

3. Using the templates, cut out each of the letters from the stamped background.

4. Hold the first letter in a large pair of tweezers and heat the surface evenly with the heat gun.

5. The plastic will shrink and thicken. When it stops contracting, turn off the heat gun.

6. Flatten the letter while it is still warm and malleable using the back of the stamp. Allow it to cool and harden.

7. Repeat for the remaining letters, and mount each one on a piece of brown card. Glue the letter to the card using strong adhesive and cut round it leaving a narrow border.

Things that make me Smile

For this page we used brown cardstock as the base. We then cut two strips of green floral-patterned paper, each with one wavy edge, and adhered them to the top and bottom edges of the page. A large photograph was attached to the centre of the design and an extra large photo corner cut from blue floral-patterned paper was positioned in the top right-hand corner.

We attached the stamped shrink-plastic title across the top of the page and die-cut tags were added down the left-hand side of the photograph. Title letters were cut from striped paper and mounted on to white card before trimming a narrow border. The design was completed with rub-on lettering on the tags and journaling strips attached randomly across the bottom of the page.

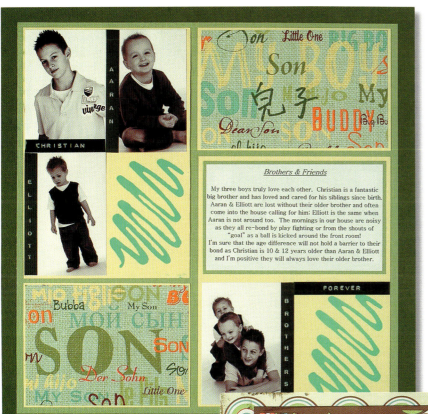

Brothers and Friends

Create simple spaces for a lot of photographs by working in blocks on the page. In this example, the page was worked as two vertical blocks which were then broken up with blocks of patterned paper that were the same size. The remaining spaces were filled with journaling, photographs and a 'squiggle' stamp.

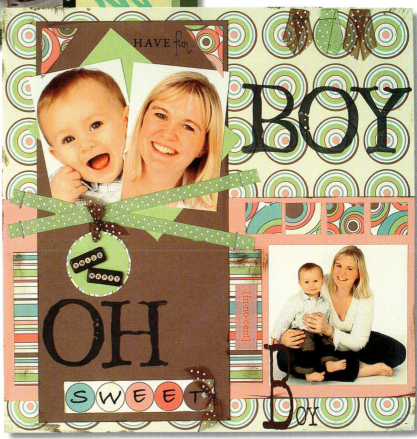

Oh Sweet Boy

A highly decorated page needs a strong title and photographs to balance the overall design. We selected very large alphabet stamps to create the title and fill all the available space.

Index

acrylic stamping block 7, 19, 26, 30, 40, 42
adhesives 10, 11, 24, 36, 41, 45
alphabet stickers 10, 15, 36, 40, 41, 44
applicators 8, 10, 30
   colour duster 10–11, 13
   cotton wool 8, 13
   crocodile-clip applicators 8, 13, 14, 34, 35, 40
   foam applicators 8, 10, 11, 12, 15, 36
   pompoms 8, 13, 14, 34, 35, 40
   stamp applicator 11, 38

brads 10, 24, 25, 30, 31, 34, 35, 40, 41, 42, 43
brayer 10, 32, 33
buttons 38, 39, 40, 41

cardstock 6, 7, 10, 15, 18, 23, 24, 25, 26, 27, 30, 31, 32, 34, 36, 38, 39, 40, 41, 42, 43, 44, 46, 48
chalk enhancer 11, 36, 37
chalks 4, 8, 10, 11, 12, 14, 30, 31, 35, 36, 37, 41
   chalk blocks 11, 30, 36, 40
   chalk inkpads 22, 26, 27
   chalk inks 8
   chalk palettes 8
   shimmer chalks 8, 34, 35, 41

die-cutting systems *see* stamp-cutting machine
direct-to-paper inking 27
dry chalking 34–35

embellishments 9–10, 22, 23, 40
embossing 8, 10, 23, 26–27, 28, 32–33
embroidery thread 38, 39, 40, 41

flowers 9, 24, 25, 40, 41, 42, 43, 44
foam brush 16, 42, 43

glitter 10, 23, 42, 43
guillotine 10, 24, 27, 44

inkpads 4, 6, 7, 8–9, 11, 16, 18, 20, 32, 42
   dye-based inkpads 24, 25
   embossing inkpads 26, 32
   pigment inkpads 14, 20, 32, 33, 44, 45
   solvent-based inkpads 40
inks 8–9, 10, 11, 12, 16, 18, 24, 32, 42, 48
   alcohol inks 9, 11, 38, 39
   dye-based inks 8, 18, 24, 25
   embossing inks 8, 26
   pigment inks 14, 33, 45
   solvent-based inks 8, 40
ironing 28–29

journaling 10, 23, 25, 31, 34, 46, 47

kissing off 8, 16, 20–21

metal letters 10, 28, 29, 32, 33

paint 9, 10, 11, 12, 16, 18, 41, 42, 43
paintbrush 10, 13, 16
paper 6, 8, 10, 12, 14, 16, 25, 27, 31, 34, 38, 39, 40, 45, 46
patterned paper 6, 12, 18, 19, 24, 26, 27, 29, 30, 31, 32, 35, 38, 39, 40, 41, 47, 48
photographs 6, 9, 10, 12, 18, 19, 22, 24, 25, 26, 27, 28, 29, 30, 31, 32, 33, 34, 35, 36, 37, 38, 39, 40, 41, 42, 43, 44, 46, 47, 48
photo mounts 10, 19, 27, 29, 33, 36, 37, 39
punches 10, 15, 28, 29, 38, 39

resist stamping 32–33
ribbons 9, 26, 27, 28, 29, 30, 31, 42, 43

rub-on lettering 10, 32, 33, 34, 35, 44, 46
rub-ons 38, 39, 43
shrink plastic 44–45, 46
soot stamping 30–31
stamp cleaning 7, 11, 16
stamp-cutting machine 7, 10, 15, 42
stamps 4, 7, 14, 16, 18, 20, 23, 24–25, 26, 28, 29, 30, 32, 47, 48
   acrylic stamps 7, 40
   foam stamps 16, 42
   mounted stamps 7, 19
   rubber stamps 7, 14, 18, 24, 26, 28, 30, 32, 44, 45
   unmounted stamps 7, 16, 19
stencils 15
storage 6, 7, 9, 10, 19

tissue paper 34, 35
trimmer *see* guillotine
twill 34, 35, 38, 39

velvet 28–29

wet chalking 36–37
word stickers 10, 32, 33

100% Boy
Repeated stamped images on plain white cardstock can create highly decorative designs that can be used in place of patterned paper.